22 Reasons Why People Fail in Property

Milan Milosevic

Published by Milan Milosevic, 2024.

22 REASONS WHY PEOPLE FAIL IN PROPERTY

First edition. April 9, 2024.

ISBN: 979-8224468669

Written by Milan Milosevic.

Table of Contents

22 REASONS WHY PEOPLE FAIL IN PROPERTY INVESTING

By Milan Milosevic

Introduction

As a Co-Founder of Riches and Beyond I didn't start where I am right now.

In fact, I made a lot of mistakes in the 14 years of my property experience while I was learning to: deal with bad tenants, broken geysers, maintenance issues, and a list of other interesting challenges.

But ultimately, I realized that it was necessary for me to go through such a diverse experience to learn what not to do to become successful. Even though my experience will always be very valuable the only problem with my journey is that it took me over 8 years to finally realize how much I didn't know.

This includes things I had to avoid or stop doing to prosper in property investing.

After finding my first multi-millionaire property mentor and discussing with him why I hadn't reached success sooner I finally concluded that there are 22 things I was doing wrong. These are available at your disposal, all of them mentioned in this study material. You will learn from them what I learned through my experience. And now you can avoid the pitfalls that other property investors unknowingly fall into, and begin to

focus on doing the right things that will help you achieve success.

I hope you will learn from my mistakes and finally get clarity on what to do to

succeed in property.

I wish you good luck and I hope to see you at the training!

To your success,

Milan Milosevic

Co-Founder Riches and Beyond

Chapter 1: Don’t know how to negotiate

From Hesitant Rookie to Real Estate Renegade

Negotiation. A single word that can evoke images of high-pressure sales rooms and fast-talking sharks circling a lone investor. But for those seeking success in the competitive world of property investment, negotiation is more than just a tactic - it's a superpower. This chapter will equip you, the aspiring real estate renegade, with the tools and knowledge to transform yourself from a hesitant rookie into a deal-closing master.

Knowledge is Power: Mastering the Market

Before entering the negotiation arena, you need to be armed with the knowledge of a market general. Here's your intel:

- **Comparable Market Analysis (CMA):** This is your bible. Research recent sales of similar properties in your target area. Is the asking price aligned with market trends? Are there external factors influencing value, like upcoming infrastructure projects or a struggling school district? A keen understanding of the market's pulse empowers you to make informed offers and counter-offers with confidence.
- **The Seller's Story:** Uncover the motivation behind the sale. Are they facing a job relocation and need a quick closing, or can they afford to wait for the perfect buyer? Understanding their urgency allows you to tailor your approach. A time-sensitive seller might be more receptive to a slightly lower offer if it means a faster sale, while a motivated seller might be open to concessions on repairs or closing costs.

Sharpening Your Negotiation Arsenal

Just like any hero, you need to train and prepare for the inevitable negotiation showdown. Here are some battle-tested tips to add to your arsenal:

- **Practice Makes Perfect:** Role-play negotiations with a friend or colleague. This allows you to anticipate counter-offers, refine your communication style, and stay calm under pressure. Imagine different scenarios: a desperate seller, a stubborn seller, a seller with unrealistic expectations. The more prepared you are, the more likely you are to emerge victorious.
- **Develop your BATNA (Best Alternative To a Negotiated Agreement):** Don't be a one-trick pony. Having a strong BATNA empowers you to walk away from a deal that doesn't meet your investment goals. It could be another property you've identified, the ability to invest in a different asset class altogether, or simply waiting for a better opportunity to arise. Knowing you have options strengthens your negotiating position and prevents you from getting emotionally attached to a particular property.

Negotiation Tactics: From Verbal Judo to Strategic Silence

Now, let's equip you with the moves to dominate the negotiation dance:

- **Become an Active Listener:** Negotiation is a two-way street. Pay close attention to the seller's responses, both verbal and nonverbal. What are their priorities? Are they hinting at flexibility on certain aspects of the deal? Can you use their needs to your advantage? Perhaps they're open to extending the closing date to allow you to secure financing, or maybe they'd rather sell quickly and are willing to contribute to some closing costs.

- **Focus on Value, Not Just Price:** While price is undeniably important, a true negotiator understands the concept of holistic value. Don't be afraid to negotiate repairs, closing costs, or even warranties on appliances. Remember, a lower purchase price doesn't always equate to a better deal. If the property requires significant renovations, factoring in those repair costs might make a seemingly good deal much less attractive.
- **Be Clear, Concise, and Professional:** When making an offer, be clear and direct, but always maintain a professional and respectful demeanor. Avoid emotional pleas or ultimatums. A confident, well-informed proposition is far more persuasive than theatrics.
- **The Power of Silence:** Silence can be a powerful tool. Don't be afraid to let the seller stew in their own thoughts after you've made your offer. It creates an opportunity for them to come back to you with a counter-offer, potentially conceding on some of your initial points.

Remember: Negotiation is a conversation, a collaborative dance between you and the seller. By understanding the market, the seller's motivations, and employing these tactics, you'll transform from a hesitant rookie into a confident investor, ready to unlock the true potential of every deal.

Bonus Tip: Consider recruiting a buyer's agent. Their experience and honed negotiation skills can be invaluable in securing the best possible outcome, saving you time, and ensuring you don't overlook any crucial details.

Now, go forth, real estate renegade! With knowledge, preparation, and a dash of negotiation savvy, you're well on your way to conquering every deal and building your property investment empire.

Chapter 2: Don't know how to find deals!

Finding Your First (and Future) Property Deals

Welcome to the thrilling world of property investment! You've crunched the numbers, you've got the financial plan locked and loaded, but there's one obstacle that looms large: finding that perfect property deal. Fear not, fellow investor, because countless beginners feel the same way. Here, we'll unveil the secrets to unearthing hidden gems and turning "I don't know where to start" into "I can't believe I found this opportunity!"

Embrace the Hustle:

Property investment is a long game, not a quick fix. Finding deals requires consistent effort. Here are a few high-impact strategies that go beyond the basic "look online":

- **Become a Market Maven:** Knowledge is power, and hyper-local knowledge is a superpower. Deep-dive into the nitty-gritty of your target area's demographics, rental yields, and property trends. Local newspapers are a goldmine for neighborhood news, while council websites often publish development plans that can hint at future property value. Don't forget industry reports and data aggregators – they can paint a broader picture of market health.
- **Network Like a Pro:** It's not just about who you know, it's about building genuine connections. Connect with other investors, real estate agents, property managers, and even local contractors. Attend industry events, join online forums specific to your target market, and don't be shy about striking up conversations at open houses. Valuable leads can come from the most unexpected places.

- **Befriend the MLS (Multiple Listing Service):** Consider the MLS your personal treasure map. Most offer powerful filters to target your ideal property type, location, and price range. However, MLS listings are just the tip of the iceberg. Don't be afraid to explore outside the platform and delve into "off-market" deals.

Go Beyond the Obvious: While traditional methods are a solid foundation, there's a whole world of "off-market" deals waiting to be discovered by the resourceful investor:

- **Direct Mail Campaigns:** Craft targeted mailers that resonate with motivated sellers who haven't yet listed their property publicly. Highlight solutions you can offer, like a quick cash sale that bypasses the hassle of a traditional listing.
- **Probate and Foreclosure Leads:** These situations often lead to property sales that move quickly. Research probate courts in your area or consider working with a realtor specializing in foreclosures.
- **"Driving for Dollars:** Get your boots on the ground! Take a literal spin through your target neighborhoods. Look for neglected properties with overgrown yards or "For Sale By Owner" signs. A friendly conversation with the owner might reveal a hidden opportunity you won't find online.

Expand Your Horizons:

Teaming up with experienced investors can be a game-changer, especially for beginners. Seasoned partners can offer valuable insights, share their hard-earned network of contacts, and even co-invest with you on promising properties. Look for local real estate investment groups or online forums where you can connect with potential collaborators.

Technology to the Rescue:

The digital age offers a wealth of online tools to streamline your search. Consider property deal sourcing platforms that aggregate off-market deals or data analysis services that identify undervalued properties based on complex algorithms. While these can be helpful resources, remember, due diligence is still crucial. Don't let fancy algorithms replace your own critical thinking and market knowledge.

Remember: Building a successful property portfolio takes time and dedication. Don't get discouraged if that perfect deal doesn't appear overnight. Be persistent, network strategically, and hone your deal-finding skills. With a proactive approach and a bit of creativity, you'll soon be a property-hunting pro, uncovering opportunities that unlock your path to financial success!

Finding deals is another theme we cover at the training so that our students know where to find deals, how to find them and how to finance them. The beautiful part with this knowledge is that stays with you forever, nobody can take it away and it gets passed down to generations.

Imagine using this knowledge ad have at least one deal per year with the

profit of over R50 000($3 000)! Would this make a difference in your life?

I am pretty sure.

But what if you have more deals than one? This is very realistic. Some of our students have done 5 deals in 5 months, 7 deals in a year, 10 deals in two years.

It is possible when you know how.

Chapter 3: Don't have the network

Conquering the Networking Challenge

Many new property investors feel overwhelmed by the idea of networking. Visions of smoke-filled rooms and awkward small talk might come to mind. But fear not! A strong network isn't about who you know, it's about **building genuine connections**. Here's how to excel in the world of property investment, even without a pre-existing network:

1. Embrace Online Communities:

The internet is a goldmine for property investors. Online forums, Facebook groups, and dedicated platforms all offer a chance to connect with like-minded individuals. These communities provide a safe space to ask questions, share experiences, and learn from seasoned investors. Actively participate in discussions, offer your own insights, and build rapport with others. Look for groups specific to your local market or investment niche. This allows you to connect with people facing similar challenges and opportunities.

2. Leverage Social Media Strategically:

Platforms like LinkedIn and Twitter are fantastic for connecting with professionals in the real estate industry. Follow real estate agents, property managers, lenders, and even successful investors. But don't just be a passive follower. Engage with their content by leaving thoughtful comments, sharing valuable articles, and participating in relevant conversations. Don't be afraid to reach out directly with a polite message introducing yourself and your goals. Tailor your message to the individual – reference something specific you liked about their work or a question you have about their area of expertise.

3. Attend Industry Events – And Make the Most of Them:

Local meetups, workshops, and conferences are fantastic opportunities to network face-to-face. However, simply attending an event isn't enough. Go prepared with an elevator pitch (a concise introduction of yourself and your goals) that's tailored to the audience. Actively seek out interesting people to connect with. Instead of just collecting business cards, strike up conversations, ask insightful questions, and find common ground. After the event, follow up with those you connected with – a quick email referencing your conversation and expressing your interest in staying in touch can go a long way.

4. Become a Resource and Establish Yourself as an Authority:

The best way to attract valuable connections is to offer value yourself. Share your knowledge by writing blog posts, creating informative videos, or even starting a local meetup group focused on a specific property investment niche. By establishing yourself as a resourceful and knowledgeable investor, you'll naturally attract others who want to learn from you. This positions you as a go-to person within your network, fostering trust and strengthening connections.

5. Focus on Building Relationships, Not Just Your Network List:

Remember, networking isn't about collecting business cards. It's about building genuine relationships. Be a good listener, show genuine interest in others, and offer help when you can. People are more likely to connect with and do business with those they trust and respect. Take the time to understand their goals and challenges. Look for ways to collaborate or offer introductions within your own network.

Bonus Tip: Start Small and Gradually Expand Your Circle:

Networking doesn't have to be overwhelming. Begin by reaching out to a few people you've met online or at an event. Schedule coffee chats or informational interviews with experienced investors. These conversations can provide valuable insights and also give you a chance to showcase your knowledge and enthusiasm. As your confidence grows, you'll find it easier to expand your network and build valuable connections. Remember, a successful network is built over time, one genuine interaction at a time.

By following these steps, you can build a strong network that will support your property investment journey. Remember, a successful network is built on trust, respect, and mutual benefit. Focus on building genuine connections, and you'll find yourself surrounded by people who can help you achieve your real estate goals.

Now imagine being part of network with over 50 000 investors which we have built with Riches and Beyond. Would this be helpful when you have potential deals? Of course!

"Build your network and your net worth will grow!"

Chapter 4: Don't work with Sourcing professionals

Why Building Your Own Network Wins Every Time

For busy property investors, the allure of a sourcing agent promising a steady stream of profitable deals can be strong. However, before you hand over your hard-earned cash, consider the hidden drawbacks and the potential benefits of cultivating your own network.

The Siren Song of Sourcing Agents

Sourcing agents position themselves as shortcuts to real estate riches. They claim to have access to exclusive, off-market properties and the expertise to navigate complex negotiations. But this convenience often comes at a steep price.

- **Opaque Fees and Potential Conflicts:** Sourcing agent fees can be hefty, often taking a significant chunk of your profit. Worse yet, some agents receive hidden commissions from sellers, creating a conflict of interest. Are they truly working for your best deal?
- **Limited Options and Missed Gems:** Sourcing agents typically focus on a specific niche or geographic area. This might restrict your access to the wider market, where hidden gems could be waiting. Building your network allows you to cast a wider net and uncover opportunities they might miss.
- **Losing Control of the Process:** By relying on an agent, you relinquish control over a crucial aspect of your investment strategy. Developing your own sourcing skills empowers you to make informed decisions based on your investment goals.

Building Your Own Deal-Flow Machine

Cultivating a strong network is an investment that pays off in the long run. Here's how to get started:

- **Become a Local Fixture:** Attend industry events, network with other investors, and connect with local brokers and property managers. Become known as a serious and reliable investor. **Go the extra mile:** Offer to help out colleagues with referrals or market insights. This fosters trust and strengthens relationships.
- **Develop Relationships with Realtors:** Build trust with realtors who understand your investment criteria. They can be a valuable source of off-market deals and early notifications. **Don't be a one-way street:** Provide value to them as well. Refer clients their way or keep them informed of potential buyers for their listings.
- **Embrace Technology:** Utilize online platforms and property databases to find potential properties. However, don't rely solely on them – personal connections are still key. **Think outside the box:** Explore social media groups or online forums dedicated to real estate investing in your target area. You might uncover hidden opportunities or connect with motivated sellers.
- **Be Patient and Persistent:** Building a network takes time and effort. Don't get discouraged if deals aren't flowing immediately. Persistence pays off in the form of a reliable stream of opportunities. **Be prepared for the long haul:**Building trust and strong relationships takes consistent interaction. Stay connected, offer help when you can, and be a valuable resource within your network.

The Rewards of Self-Sourcing

The legwork of building your network is well worth the rewards. Here's what you gain:

- **Deeper Market Knowledge:** By immersing yourself in the local market, you develop a keen sense of property values and upcoming trends. This allows you to identify undervalued properties with high potential. You'll be able to spot deals that sourcing agents might miss because you have a finger on the pulse of the local market.
- **Greater Control and Flexibility:** You control the deal flow and tailor your sourcing strategy to your specific investment goals. No more being restricted by an agent's limited scope. **Want to invest in a specific neighborhood?** Build relationships with local residents and property managers in that area. They can be your eyes and ears on the ground, keeping you informed about potential opportunities.
- **Building Long-Term Relationships:** The connections you build become a valuable asset. They can be a source of future deals, referrals, and valuable insights. **Your network is your net worth:** When you invest in building strong relationships, you create a support system that can benefit you throughout your investing career. They can be a sounding board for ideas, a source of moral support during challenging times, and a springboard for future collaborations.

The Bottom Line

While sourcing agents can be tempting shortcuts, the potential drawbacks often outweigh the benefits for property investors. By investing time and effort in building your own network, you gain control, flexibility, and deeper market knowledge. Remember, the best deals are often found through connections, not from a one-size-fits-all agent. So, roll up your sleeves, network strategically, and become your own deal-finding machine. The legwork you put in today will pave the way for a successful and profitable future in real estate investing.

Chapter 5: Don’t have a mentor

Learn from people more successful than you

The dream of a property mentor – a seasoned investor who guides you through the intricate world of real estate – is a powerful one. But what if that's not your reality? Fear not, aspiring landlord! Building a successful portfolio is absolutely achievable without a mentor by your side. Here's how to navigate the path to property ownership independently:

1. Knowledge is Power: Become a Real Estate Bookworm

The information age is your greatest ally. Dive headfirst into property investment books, online courses, and reputable websites. Look for resources that cover the investment strategies you're interested in, whether it's buy-to-let, flips, or rentals. Don't just stick to traditional textbooks. Explore podcasts, webinars, and YouTube channels run by successful investors. Many offer valuable insights and practical advice gleaned from their own experiences.

2. Network Like a Pro: Find Your Tribe

While you may not have a single mentor, there's a wealth of knowledge waiting to be tapped in property investor communities. Join online forums dedicated to real estate investing. Look for local meetups or groups on platforms like Meetup.com or Facebook. Actively participate in discussions, ask questions, and share your experiences. You'll be surprised by the willingness of others to help and share their knowledge. We have built The Property Game Tribe, the largest property investors network with over 50 000 investors and mentors in one place to assist solo property investors.

3. Shadow the Experts: Invest in Education

Consider attending real estate workshops and conferences. These events offer the chance to learn from experienced investors and industry professionals. Take advantage of Q&A sessions to gain specific insights and address your concerns about your chosen investment strategy or a particular property you're considering. Look for workshops with a focus on areas you might lack experience in, such as property valuation, legal considerations, or tenant management. Starting with free webinars and all the way to weekend masterclasses plus specific tailor made mentorships, Riches and Beyond has become the leading property educational company in South Africa and globally.

4. Analyze, Analyze, Analyze: Develop Your Research Skills

A mentor can't replace your own due diligence. Hone your research skills to analyze potential properties. Learn how to interpret market trends using resources like government reports and industry publications. Assess rental yields by researching comparable properties in the area. Utilize online tools like property valuation websites and heatmaps to get a sense of market value and rental potential. Don't be afraid to get your hands dirty physically visit neighborhoods you're interested in to get a feel for the area and its amenities.

5. Find Your Support System: Build a Team of Experts

While you may not have a single mentor, surround yourself with a team of reliable professionals. This could include a real estate agent who specializes in the type of property you're looking for, a property manager to handle tenant issues and day-to-day operations, a lawyer specializing in real estate to ensure contracts are sound and protect your interests, and a qualified accountant who can advise on tax implications and optimize your investment strategy.

6. Learn from the Mistakes of Others: Case Studies are Your Friends

Read case studies of successful (and unsuccessful) property investors. Analyze their strategies, identify common pitfalls, and learn from their triumphs and tribulations. Look for case studies that align with your investment goals. Are you interested in flipping houses? Read about investors who specialize in renovations and quick sales. Do you want to build a rental portfolio for long-term income? Find case studies that showcase buy-to-let strategies and property management techniques. Many real estate websites and online communities feature investor stories – use them as valuable learning tools.

7. Embrace Calculated Risks: Don't Be Afraid to Start Small

Don't wait for the "perfect" opportunity or the elusive mentor. Start small with a property that fits your budget and risk tolerance. A smaller investment can be a stepping stone to bigger things. Consider a duplex or a single-family home as your first property. This allows you to gain experience in property management and renovations (if needed) on a smaller scale before tackling larger multi-unit buildings.

The Takeaway: Learn from the Best

Building a successful property portfolio without a mentor requires initiative, dedication, and a willingness to learn. The most rewarding part is learning from someone who has made mistakes so that you don't have to. However, the rewards can be substantial. By becoming a guided investor, you'll develop a unique skillset and gain valuable confidence in your decision-making. Remember, the journey of a thousand miles begins with a single step. So, take that first step, embrace the learning curve, and build your property empire brick by brick. You might even find yourself becoming a mentor to others along the way. With Top Residential property investments mentors with

Riches and Beyond, you can be sure to find the right fit for your property journey.

Chapter 6 : Do it Yourself rabbit hole

Saving money or costly mistakes

The allure of DIY (Do-It-Yourself) is strong for property investors. It offers the promise of saving money on repairs and renovations, fostering a sense of accomplishment, and gaining a deeper understanding of your investment. But before you grab your toolbox, consider this: There's a fine line between savvy self-sufficiency and turning a minor fix into a major headache.

The ROI of DIY

Let's be honest, there's a certain satisfaction in tackling a project yourself and seeing it through. However, the true return on investment (ROI) of DIY hinges on two key factors:

- **Your Skillset:** Be brutally honest about your abilities. Are you a natural handyman, or do your attempts at fixing a leaky faucet lead to a flooded bathroom? Consider taking online courses or attending workshops to hone your skills before diving into complex projects.
- **Project Complexity:** Some tasks, like painting a wall or replacing a light fixture, are perfect for DIY beginners. On the other hand, rewiring an electrical system or undertaking structural repairs are best left to licensed professionals. Don't be afraid to consult with contractors or handymen for an initial assessment to gauge the complexity of a project before deciding to DIY.

When DIY Makes Dollars and Sense

There are numerous situations where DIY shines for property investors:

- **Cosmetic Refreshments:** A fresh coat of paint, new cabinet hardware, or updated light fixtures can significantly enhance a property's appeal without requiring extensive expertise. DIYing these projects allows you to personalize the space to your target tenant or buyer and potentially command higher rents or a better sale price.
- **Minor Repairs:** Leaky faucets, sticking doors, or loose doorknobs are common issues that can often be addressed with a little elbow grease and readily available tools. Not only does DIY save money on repair costs, but it also ensures your tenants have a comfortable and functional living space, reducing the likelihood of maintenance requests.
- **Preventative Maintenance:** Simple tasks like cleaning gutters, replacing air filters, and checking smoke detectors can prevent costly problems down the road. Taking a proactive approach to maintenance through DIY not only saves money but also demonstrates to tenants that you're a responsible landlord who cares about the condition of the property.

Knowing When to Call in the Pros

Don't be afraid to step back and recognize when a project is beyond your capabilities. Here are some red flags:

- **Safety Concerns:** Electrical work, plumbing, and anything involving structural integrity should be left to licensed professionals. There's no shame in prioritizing safety over saving a few bucks. A single mistake in these areas could result in serious injury, property damage, or even legal repercussions.
- **Lack of Confidence:** If you're unsure about how to proceed,

even after consulting online resources or tutorials, it's better to seek guidance from an expert. A botched DIY attempt can be far more expensive to rectify than hiring a professional from the outset.

- **Time Constraints:** Being a property investor often means juggling multiple properties and tenant needs. If time is limited, entrusting a project to a professional can free you to focus on other priorities like tenant screening, market research, or securing new investment opportunities.

The Golden Rule: Research and Preparation

Even for seemingly straightforward DIY projects, thorough research and preparation are key. Here are some tips to maximize your success:

- **Consult Online Resources:** There's a wealth of informative websites and video tutorials offering step-by-step guides for DIY tasks. Utilize online resources to not only understand the process but also learn from the experiences of others. Watch multiple tutorials to get a well-rounded understanding of the task before starting.
- **Gather the Right Tools:** Having the necessary tools for the job will make the process smoother and more efficient. Don't invest in expensive tools you'll only use once; consider renting for specialized jobs. Many hardware stores offer tool rental programs, allowing you to access professional-grade equipment without a hefty upfront investment.
- **Start Small, Scale Up Gradually:** Build your confidence by tackling smaller projects before graduating to more complex ones. This allows you to develop your skills and gain experience in a low-risk environment. As you gain confidence, you can gradually take on more challenging tasks.

The Takeaway

DIY can be a powerful tool for property investors. By understanding your skillset, carefully assessing project complexity, and prioritizing safety, you can leverage DIY to save money, enhance your properties, and gain valuable knowledge. Remember, there's no shame in calling in the pros when necessary. A successful property investor knows when to roll up their sleeves and when to step back and delegate. By employing this strategic approach, you can ensure your DIY projects contribute to your overall investment success.

Chapter 7: Using cheap labour

Why Cheap Can Cost You Dear

In the fast-paced world of property investment, keeping costs down is a constant quest. But when it comes to labour, sacrificing quality for rock-bottom prices can backfire spectacularly. Here, we explore the hidden dangers of relying solely on cheap labour for your property projects:

1. Quality Cuts: A Recipe for Repair Bills

Skilled labour might seem expensive upfront, but it ensures the job is done right the first time. Cheap labour often translates to a lack of experience, leading to shortcuts, missed building codes, and ultimately, repairs down the line. These repairs can cost significantly more than the initial saving on labour, not to mention the inconvenience and potential delays. Imagine replacing a poorly installed plumbing system throughout a building – a nightmare scenario easily avoided by investing in a qualified plumber from the outset.

2. The Revolving Door of Inexperience

Cheap labour often comes with a high turnover rate. Inexperienced workers might be more likely to leave for slightly better pay elsewhere, leaving you scrambling to find replacements and constantly retraining new hires. This disrupts project timelines, impacting your overall budget and rental income potential. Consistency is key in property investment. A reliable team you can develop a working relationship with ensures a smooth workflow, fewer mistakes, and ultimately, a higher quality project.

3. Communication Breakdowns & Legal Nightmares

Language barriers and a lack of clear communication can be disastrous when dealing with complex repairs or renovations. Misunderstandings can lead to incorrect installations, safety hazards, and even legal issues if building codes are not followed. Invest in clear communication and qualified professionals to avoid these costly headaches. For instance, improper electrical work due to miscommunication can lead to fires, injuries, and even legal ramifications. Don't let misunderstandings turn your investment into a liability.

4. Safety Concerns: A Recipe for Disaster

Cutting corners on labour can have serious safety repercussions. Inexperienced workers might not be properly trained on safety protocols, increasing the risk of accidents and injuries. This can lead to lawsuits, project delays, and damage to your reputation as a property investor. Prioritize safety by ensuring your contractors have a proven track record of adhering to safety regulations. This protects your workers, your property, and your investment.

5. The Domino Effect of Delays

Cheap labour often translates to slow, inefficient work. Workers might lack the proper tools or training, leading to delays that push back your project timeline. This can have a domino effect, impacting rental income, tenant satisfaction, and potentially even future financing opportunities. Reliable, skilled workers tend to be efficient, completing tasks to a high standard and within the agreed timeframe. This allows you to get your property rented out sooner and start generating a return on your investment.

The Ethical Investment Advantage

While cost is a concern, remember that your property is an investment. Paying fair wages attracts skilled and reliable workers who take pride in their craft. This leads to higher quality work, fewer problems down the road, and a property that retains its value over time. Additionally, ethical treatment of workers fosters positive word-of-mouth, potentially attracting better tenants and creating a win-win situation. Building positive relationships with contractors based on mutual respect and fair compensation lays the foundation for successful projects and a strong reputation as a property investor. In the long run, investing in quality people translates into a quality investment property.

Chapter 8: Hope prices will increase

Why Waiting for Appreciation Isn't a Strategy

The allure of real estate is undeniable. It's a tangible asset, a source of rental income, and – ideally – an appreciating investment. But for many new investors, the focus becomes solely on the appreciation aspect, leading to a dangerous strategy: the hope gamble.

This chapter dives into the pitfalls of relying solely on price increases and explores alternative approaches to ensure your property investment journey is built on a solid foundation.

The Faulty Logic of the Hope Gamble

The hope gamble hinges on the belief that as long as you hold onto a property, its value will inevitably rise. This can be true in some cases, particularly in booming markets. However, it's a gamble nonetheless. The property market is cyclical, with periods of growth followed by corrections. Basing your entire investment strategy on the hope of future appreciation exposes you to significant risks:

- **Missed Opportunities:** While you wait for a potential price hike, you might miss out on acquiring properties with better immediate returns, like strong rental yields. These returns can be re-invested to grow your portfolio faster, or provide a financial buffer during economic downturns.
- **Market Downturns:** Unexpected economic downturns can cause property values to stagnate or even decline. This can leave you stuck with an illiquid asset that's worth less than your purchase price. Not only does this wipe out any potential profit, but it can also restrict your ability to access capital to invest elsewhere.

- **Opportunity Cost:** The money you tie up in a property hoping for appreciation could be invested elsewhere, generating a more predictable return. Diversifying your investments across asset classes like stocks or bonds can provide a hedge against market downturns and offer a more balanced risk-reward profile.

Building a Sustainable Investment Strategy

Instead of relying on hope, here are key elements to consider for a robust property investment strategy:

- **Cash Flow is King:** Prioritize properties that generate positive cash flow from rental income. This provides a steady return even if market appreciation is slow. A positive cash flow property acts like a well-oiled machine, consistently putting money in your pocket, which can be used to reinvest in further acquisitions or pay down debt.
- **Location, Location, Location:** Invest in areas with strong rental demand, appreciating demographics, and future development potential. These factors contribute to long-term value growth. Look for areas with a healthy mix of residential and commercial properties, good infrastructure, and a growing job market. These areas tend to attract tenants and provide a strong foundation for rental income and future capital appreciation.
- **The Power of Research:** Don't just hope for the best, do your homework. Research market trends, understand local rental yields, and factor in potential maintenance costs. By thoroughly researching a property and its surroundings, you can avoid overpaying and ensure you're making a sound investment decision.

- **Diversification is Key:** Spread your investments across different property types or locations to mitigate risk and capture opportunities in diverse market segments. Consider investing in a mix of residential and commercial properties, or diversifying geographically across different cities or regions. This helps mitigate risk by ensuring you're not overly exposed to a downturn in any one market.

Remember: Appreciation is a bonus, not a guarantee. By focusing on strong fundamentals like cash flow and strategic acquisition, you can build a resilient property portfolio that weathers market fluctuations and delivers consistent returns.

The takeaway? Be a savvy investor, not a hopeful gambler. Let informed decisions, not wishful thinking, guide your property investment journey.

Through training we teach our students how to make money from property

when the market is going up and when it's down.

Chapter 9: Try to make money when they sell, not when they buy

Why Focusing on Entry Makes You More Money

In the fast-paced world of property investment, the allure of a quick sale at a high price can be intoxicating. However, seasoned investors know a crucial truth: the real money is made when you buy, not when you sell. This chapter dives into the pitfalls of the "sell high" mentality and explores why focusing on acquiring the right property at the right price is the foundation of sustainable property wealth.

The Delusion of "Selling High"

Imagine this scenario: you find a property that seems slightly overpriced, but you convince yourself the market will rise soon, allowing you to flip it for a hefty profit. This gamble hinges on two external factors, both fraught with peril:

1. **Market Timing:** Predicting market peaks and troughs is notoriously difficult, akin to catching a falling knife. Even a seemingly small miscalculation can leave you holding an appreciating (but illiquid) asset or worse, stuck with a depreciating one that struggles to find buyers.
2. **Unforeseen Events:** Economic downturns, interest rate fluctuations, and unexpected changes in the local market, like a new bypass road diverting traffic away from a commercial property, can derail your flipping strategy entirely.

The Power of the Right Entry Point

Shrewd investors prioritize properties with strong fundamentals that position them for success irrespective of short-term market gyrations:

- **Location, Location, Location:** This mantra remains a

cornerstone of property investment wisdom for a reason. Focus on areas with consistent demand, good infrastructure, and a growing population. These areas are more likely to experience steady price appreciation over time, driven by organic market forces.

- **Property Type:** Analyze market trends to identify property types with high rental yields or strong capital growth potential. For example, a growing city with a limited housing supply might make apartments a good bet, while a tourist destination might favor vacation rentals.
- **Underlying Value:** Look beyond the surface and identify properties with hidden potential. Perhaps a fixer-upper in a desirable neighbourhood offers a chance to add value through renovation, or a commercial property with a long-term lease to a stable tenant provides a secure income stream.

By securing a well-priced property with inherent value, you create a buffer against market fluctuations. Even in a stagnant market, you'll benefit from:

- **Rental Income:** A well-chosen property, ideally tenanted by credit-worthy renters, generates a steady stream of rental income, providing a positive cash flow from day one. This income can be used to cover your mortgage payment, build equity, and potentially reinvest in further properties.
- **Long-Term Appreciation:** While you can't control the market, buying in a strong location with solid fundamentals increases the chances of your property appreciating over time. This long-term growth contributes significantly to your overall wealth creation strategy.

Beyond the Bottom Line

Focusing on entry strategy isn't just about financial gain. It also reduces the stress and uncertainty of the selling process. When you buy right, you're more likely to attract qualified buyers who recognize the inherent value of your property – a well-maintained property in a desirable location with strong rental potential. This translates into a smoother selling experience, potentially with multiple offers and a sale at (or above) market value.

Remember: Property investment is a marathon, not a sprint. By prioritizing a strategic purchase over a quick sale, you lay the foundation for long-term wealth creation and a less stressful property ownership experience. The next chapter will explore strategies for finding those undervalued gems and negotiating the best possible entry price, giving you the upper hand from the very beginning of your property investment journey.

You can make money using specific skills, techniques and learned knowledge.

to acquire property below market value.

Why, because numbers just make more sense when property is bought below market value.

And this is one of the most important lessons we teach at our training.

Chapter 10: Doesn't invest in the cashflow

Why Ignoring Cashflow Can Sink Your Property Portfolio

For many property investors, the allure lies in bricks and mortar – a tangible asset that delivers a steady stream of rental income. But what if that stream turns into a trickle, or worse, dries up entirely? This is the harsh reality that awaits investors who prioritize headline figures like purchase price and potential capital appreciation over the lifeblood of any investment: cashflow.

This chapter dives into the critical mistakes that can arise from neglecting cashflow in your property investment strategy.

Mistake #1: Focusing on Paper Profits, Ignoring Cold Hard Cash

Many beginners fall prey to the illusion of profit on paper. They project future sale prices and factor in potential appreciation, neglecting the actual money coming in each month. Remember, a property you can't afford to maintain or that sits vacant isn't generating income, and a negative cashflow property can quickly drain your resources. Let's say you purchase a property with the expectation that its value will rise significantly in a few years. While appreciation is a potential benefit, it shouldn't be the sole focus. If the property produces negative cashflow in the meantime, you'll be constantly feeding money into a black hole. This can significantly strain your finances and limit your ability to invest in other opportunities.

Mistake #2: Underestimating Expenses: It's Not Just About Rent

When calculating cashflow, factor in ALL expenses, not just the mortgage. Taxes, maintenance, insurance, vacancy periods, and even property management fees all eat into your profits. A common underestimation is repairs – unexpected issues like a burst pipe or a failing roof can blow a hole in your budget. Don't be caught off guard! Budget realistically for ongoing maintenance and repairs, including potential replacements for major appliances like the HVAC system. Building a buffer for unexpected costs will ensure your cashflow remains positive.

Mistake #3: Ignoring the Impact of Vacancy

Rental properties aren't occupied 100% of the time. Factor in vacancy periods when calculating cashflow. Analyze historical vacancy rates in your target area and budget accordingly. Remember, even a short vacancy can significantly impact your cashflow. Consider offering competitive rent, providing a well-maintained property, and having a streamlined tenant screening process to minimize vacancy periods.

Mistake #4: Not Building a Cashflow Buffer

Life throws curveballs. Unexpected repairs, tenant issues, or even interest rate hikes can disrupt your carefully planned cashflow. Build a buffer by having a healthy emergency fund specifically for your property portfolio. This financial cushion will ensure you can weather storms without jeopardizing your investment. Imagine a scenario where your star tenant gives notice unexpectedly. Having a cashflow buffer allows you to cover the mortgage and other expenses while you find a new tenant, preventing a financial hardship.

Investing for the Long Term: The Power of Positive Cashflow

By prioritizing cashflow, you're building a sustainable property portfolio with several advantages:

- **Cashflow-Positive Properties:** Seek properties that generate income that exceeds your total expenses. This positive cashflow allows you to reinvest in your portfolio or build wealth through passive income. Let's say you own two properties: one with a negative cashflow and another with a positive cashflow. The positive cashflow from the second property can help offset the negative cashflow from the first, while also generating additional income you can use to invest in a third property, further expanding your portfolio and increasing your wealth.

- **Flexibility and Growth:** A strong cashflow provides flexibility. You can weather market downturns, make strategic purchases during economic slowdowns, or even retire comfortably with a steady stream of rental income. Imagine a scenario where the housing market experiences a downturn. With positive cashflow from your properties, you're not forced to sell at a loss. You have the breathing room to ride out the storm and potentially even use the downturn to your advantage by acquiring additional properties at a discount.
- **Peace of Mind:** Positive cashflow brings peace of mind. You know your rentals are covering their expenses and generating additional income. This allows you to focus on the bigger picture of your investment strategy and avoid the constant worry of potential shortfalls.

Remember, property investment is a marathon, not a sprint. By prioritizing cashflow, you're laying the foundation for a secure financial future that weathers market fluctuations and builds wealth over time.

Chapter 11: Think they know everything

Why You Don't Know Everything (And That's Okay)

In the fast-paced world of property investment, confidence is key. But there's a fine line between that and the Dunning-Kruger effect – a cognitive bias where someone with limited knowledge overestimates their competence. Here's why recognizing this pitfall is crucial for building a sustainable property portfolio.

The Illusion of Expertise:

Imagine a new investor, eager and fresh out of a real estate seminar. They might feel they possess all the knowledge needed to navigate the market. This initial confidence can be dangerous. The reality is, property investment is a complex game with ever-shifting variables – market trends, legalities, maintenance costs, and tenant dynamics, just to name a few. An experienced investor understands that the learning curve is constant, and there's always new knowledge to be gained.

The Dangers of Dunning-Kruger:

- **Missed Opportunities:** Overconfidence can blind you to valuable learning opportunities. You might dismiss expert advice from a seasoned broker or miss crucial market indicators because you believe you already have it all figured out. This can lead to overlooking hidden gems or missing out on advantageous deals.
- **Poor Decision-Making:** Misjudging your knowledge can lead to hasty decisions. You might rush into an unsuitable property, swayed by emotional appeal or surface-level factors, only to discover hidden problems down the line. Overconfidence can also lead to neglecting critical factors

during negotiations, potentially costing you thousands on the purchase price or rental terms.

- **Limited Growth:** Believing you know everything shuts the door on growth. A true expert is constantly learning, adapting, and refining their approach. The property market is fluid, and what worked yesterday might not work tomorrow. By staying closed off to new knowledge and perspectives, you limit your ability to adapt and potentially miss out on lucrative opportunities.

Embracing the "I Don't Know" Mindset:

The good news is, the antidote to Dunning-Kruger is readily available: humility. Here's how to cultivate a healthy "I don't know" mindset:

- **Seek Mentorship:** Find experienced investors or advisors willing to share their knowledge. Look for individuals with a proven track record and a willingness to guide you through the intricacies of the market. Ask questions, learn from their mistakes, and leverage their experience to avoid costly pitfalls.
- **Continuous Learning:** The property market is dynamic. Stay updated on industry trends, legal changes, and investment strategies through courses, workshops, and market reports. Numerous resources are available online and through professional organizations. Dedicate time to expanding your knowledge base – it's an investment that will pay off handsomely in the long run.
- **Embrace Diverse Perspectives:** Don't be afraid to seek out different viewpoints. Talk to other investors, tenants, and property managers. A well-rounded perspective minimizes blind spots. An experienced tenant might offer valuable insights into what makes a desirable rental property, while a

property manager can shed light on the realities of property upkeep and tenant management.

- **Step Outside Your Comfort Zone:** Challenge yourself to explore unfamiliar territory. Consider different property types, locations, or investment strategies. This will broaden your knowledge base and potentially uncover hidden opportunities you might have otherwise overlooked.

Remember:

Acknowledging you don't have all the answers isn't a weakness – it's a strength. It opens the door to continuous learning, growth, and ultimately, smarter investments. By embracing a growth mindset, you'll be well on your way to becoming a truly knowledgeable and successful property investor. The journey to property investment mastery is a lifelong pursuit, and those who embrace the "I don't know" mentality are the ones who will reap the greatest rewards.

Chapter 12: Don't know the numbers

Why Number Crunching is King in Property Investment

Welcome, property investors! The thrill of the hunt, the satisfaction of a successful deal – these are just some of the reasons we're drawn to this exciting field. But let's face it, emotions can cloud judgment. And in the world of real estate, where figures reign supreme, a shaky grasp on the numbers can lead to costly mistakes.

This chapter dives deep into the perils of number neglect, highlighting common pitfalls and equipping you with the knowledge to avoid them.

Beyond ROI: Unveiling the Investment Trifecta

While ROI is a crucial metric, it's just one piece of the puzzle. Savvy investors understand the power of the "investment trifecta": cash flow, appreciation, and tax benefits.

- **Cash Flow:** This is the lifeblood of your investment. It represents the net income generated by your property after accounting for all expenses. Positive cash flow ensures your investment generates ongoing income, not just a future lump sum.
- **Appreciation:** Ideally, the value of your property should increase over time. Understanding market trends and property types with strong growth potential allows you to factor in potential appreciation when calculating your overall return.
- **Tax Benefits:** Real estate offers a variety of tax advantages that can significantly improve your bottom line. Depreciation deductions, mortgage interest tax deductions, and potential tax breaks for specific property types can all boost your

returns.

Understanding how these three elements work together paints a more comprehensive picture of your investment's true potential.

Beyond Spreadsheets: Building Your Financial Fortress

Financial modeling is powerful, but it's just one tool in your arsenal. Building a strong financial foundation is essential for navigating the complexities of real estate investment. Here's how to go beyond basic calculations:

- **Secure a Solid Funding Strategy:** Cash purchases might seem ideal, but leverage can be a powerful tool when used strategically. Explore financing options, understand loan terms, and factor in potential interest rate fluctuations.
- **Build a Cash Reserve:** Unexpected expenses are inevitable. Maintain a healthy cash reserve to cover repairs, vacancies, and market downturns. This financial buffer ensures you can weather unforeseen storms.
- **Develop a Team of Experts:** A qualified accountant, realtor, and property manager can be invaluable assets. Their expertise can help you navigate complex financial scenarios, identify profitable opportunities, and ensure your investment runs smoothly.

By combining financial literacy with strategic planning, you'll transform yourself from a number-crunching novice into a confident investor, making informed decisions that secure your financial future.

Remember, successful real estate investment is a marathon, not a sprint. By prioritizing a deep understanding of the numbers, coupled with sound financial planning, you'll be well on your way to reaping the rewards of a lucrative and fulfilling property portfolio.

If numbers make sense, we go for it. If not, we step away. There is always another deal!

Chapter 13: Going Solo without the team

The Pitfalls of Ignoring the Mastermind Team

In the thrilling world of property investment, venturing forth as a lone wolf can hold a certain romantic appeal. The idea of forging your own path, relying solely on your own grit and determination, is undeniably attractive. But before you cast aside the notion of a "mastermind team" altogether, consider this: even the most skilled hunters operate with a pack for a reason.

This chapter will delve into the perils of going solo in property investment and the undeniable advantages of assembling a team of experts.

The Lone Wolf's Lament: Common Mistakes

- **Knowledge Gaps:** Property investment encompasses a vast landscape – legalities, market trends, financing, renovations, tenant management – the list goes on. A single individual simply cannot be an authority on all fronts. A mastermind team, with each member bringing their specialized knowledge, fills these critical gaps. Imagine trying to diagnose a complex car problem yourself. You might be able to muddle through, but a mechanic with specialized training and tools can identify the issue quickly and efficiently. The same logic applies to property investment.
- **Tunnel Vision:** Being overly invested (pun intended) in your own perspective can lead to missed opportunities and blind spots. A team brings diverse viewpoints to the table, fostering a more holistic approach to decision-making. Let's say you're set on a particular location based on current rental rates. A teammate with an eye for future development trends might

point out upcoming infrastructure projects that could significantly impact that area's long-term value. This kind of diverse perspective can help you make well-rounded choices.

- **The Echo Chamber:** Surrounding yourself solely with those who confirm your existing beliefs can be detrimental. A good team provides honest feedback, challenging assumptions and prompting you to consider alternative strategies. Perhaps you're convinced a certain renovation project will significantly boost your rental income. A contractor on your team might offer a reality check, suggesting more cost-effective ways to achieve the same outcome. This kind of honest feedback can save you time, money, and frustration.
- **The Information Abyss:** The sheer volume of information available online can be overwhelming. A team with established networks and experience can curate valuable resources, saving you from information overload. Imagine trying to navigate an unfamiliar city with only a basic map. You might eventually reach your destination, but it would be a slow and inefficient process. A local teammate, familiar with the city's layout, can point you in the right direction quickly and efficiently. In the same way, a team with experience in your target market can guide you to the most relevant and reliable sources of information.
- **The Negotiation Maze:** Skilled negotiators can significantly impact your bottom line. Whether it's securing a favorable purchase price or navigating tenant negotiations, a team with expertise in this area is invaluable. Negotiating a real estate deal can be a complex dance. An experienced agent on your team can anticipate the seller's counteroffers, formulate strategic responses, and ultimately secure a better deal for you.

Building Your Mastermind Team: Key Players

- **The Real Estate Agent:** A good agent is more than just a middleman. They possess in-depth local market knowledge, negotiation skills, and connections within the industry. Think of them as your trusted guide through the often-murky waters of the real estate market.
- **The Mortgage Broker:** Securing the right financing is crucial. A skilled mortgage broker can navigate complex loan options and secure the best terms for your investment. They act as your financial translator, ensuring you understand the nuances of different loan products and choose the one that best suits your investment goals.
- **The Lawyer:** Legal complexities abound in property investment. Having a lawyer on your team ensures your deals are legally sound and protects your interests. They act as your shield, safeguarding you from potential legal pitfalls that could derail your investment.
- **The Property Inspector:** Unforeseen property issues can derail your investment. A thorough property inspection by a qualified professional is essential. They act as your eyes and ears, uncovering hidden problems that could cost you dearly down the line.
- **The Property Manager (Optional):** For those new to property management, a reliable property manager can alleviate the stress of tenant screening, rent collection, and maintenance headaches. They act as your boots on the ground, handling the day-to-day operations of your investment property and freeing you to focus on growing your portfolio.

The Synergy Effect: The Power of Collaboration

The true magic of a mastermind team lies in the synergy it creates. Each member brings their expertise, experience, and network, fostering a collaborative environment that empowers you to achieve far more than you could alone.

Consider this: while you may have a keen eye for potential properties, your real estate agent can leverage their local knowledge to uncover

Chapter 14: Don't have the right knowledge

Why You Don't Know What You Don't Know (And Why That's Okay)

Congratulations! You've taken the exciting first step towards building wealth through property investment. But before you get swept up in the thrill of the hunt, let's address a crucial aspect: knowledge.

The allure of real estate is undeniable. Success stories abound, and the promise of passive income can be intoxicating. However, many aspiring investors dive in without fully understanding the intricacies of the market. They might have seen a few headlines or believe it's a simple "buy low, sell high" scenario. This lack of knowledge can lead to costly mistakes, missed opportunities, and ultimately, a portfolio that underperforms.

Here's why acknowledging the knowledge gap is essential:

- **Beyond the Purchase Price:** Real estate transactions involve a financial labyrinth beyond the initial purchase price. Closing costs, property taxes, ongoing maintenance, potential vacancies – these factors can significantly impact your cash flow. Without understanding them, you can be blindsided by unexpected expenses that erode your profit margin.
- **Location, Location, Location (and Market Dynamics):** Every market is unique, with its own set of variables. Overestimating rental income based on national averages in a specific neighborhood, or underestimating renovation costs due to a lack of understanding of local contractor rates, can throw your entire financial plan into disarray. Knowing how to analyze market trends, property values, and rental yields is crucial for making informed investment decisions.
- **The Legal Landscape:** Real estate is not just about bricks

and mortar; it involves a web of legalities. Tenant rights and lease agreements, zoning regulations and building codes – unfamiliarity with these can lead to legal disputes, costly fines, and even potential eviction headaches down the line.

Now, here's the good news: Admitting the knowledge gap is not a weakness; it's the first step to success. Here's how to bridge it:

- **Become a Knowledge Sponge:** Immerse yourself in the world of real estate. Devour books, articles, and blogs written by reputable investors. Take online courses, attend workshops, and join investor groups or forums. Surround yourself with knowledge and insights from those who have walked the path before you.
- **Seek Mentorship:** Find experienced investors who can guide you. A good mentor can share their knowledge, offer valuable advice, and help you avoid common pitfalls. Look for someone whose investment philosophy aligns with yours, and who is willing to answer your questions and provide ongoing support.
- **Learn by Doing (Cautiously):** Don't be afraid to take action. However, remember the old adage: "measure twice, cut once." Start small. Consider investing in a more modest property initially, or partner with a more experienced investor on your first deal. This allows you to gain practical experience, build your confidence, and minimize risk while you continue to learn and refine your investment strategy.

Remember, knowledge is power. By actively seeking education, mentorship, and practical experience, you can transform the knowledge gap into a springboard for success. The more you learn, the more confident you'll be in making sound investment decisions, building a robust portfolio, and ultimately, achieving your financial goals through property investment.

Bonus Tip: Utilize Free Resources! The good news is you don't have to break the bank to bridge your knowledge gap. Many valuable resources are available for free. Local libraries often have a wealth of books and publications on real estate investing. Your local government website might offer resources on zoning regulations and permitting processes. Online, there are countless free webinars, podcasts, and Youtube channels hosted by experienced investors offering insights and strategies. Take advantage of these resources to jumpstart your learning journey.

Chapter 15: Analysis - Paralysis

From Procrastination to Property Powerhouse

The thrill of the hunt! You've decided to invest in property, a fantastic decision that can build long-term wealth and security. But wait. What if the market dips? Is this the right location? What about hidden repair costs? Suddenly, excitement curdles into overwhelming doubt. You're stuck in analysis paralysis, a state where information overload leads to inaction. Fear not, fellow investor, this chapter equips you to break free and make powerful property decisions.

The Perils of Procrastination

Analysis paralysis isn't just about missing out on deals. It can:

- **Cost you money:** Prime properties get snapped up quickly. While you're endlessly analyzing spreadsheets, decisive investors are building their portfolios and reaping the benefits of appreciation.
- **Fuel frustration:** The longer you stay stagnant, the more the dream of property ownership can feel out of reach, leading to discouragement and a sense of powerlessness.
- **Hinder learning:** Real estate wisdom comes from experience, not just from textbooks. By taking calculated risks and making decisions, you gain valuable insights that future analysis will be built upon. You'll learn to identify good deals, assess potential problems, and navigate the complexities of the market – all through the invaluable lessons of experience.

Shifting From Stagnation to Strategic Action

Here's your action plan to move from analysis to acquisition:

- **Set SMART Goals:** Specific, Measurable, Achievable, Relevant, and Time-bound goals provide a clear roadmap. Define your investment criteria (location, type, budget) and a timeframe for your first purchase. Don't get bogged down in endless possibilities – focus on what aligns with your overall financial goals.
- **Embrace Imperfect Information:** The property market is dynamic. You won't have all the answers beforehand, and waiting for perfect information can be a recipe for inaction. Rely on your research, trusted advisors, and be prepared to adapt as you learn. Develop a tolerance for ambiguity – it's part of the investment landscape.
- **Timebox Your Analysis:** Allocate a specific time frame for research (e.g., 2 weeks) and stick to it. Don't let the pursuit of perfect information become an excuse for inaction. Set deadlines and hold yourself accountable.
- **Focus on Action:** There will always be "what ifs." Shift your mindset from analyzing every possibility to taking the first step, like scheduling property viewings. Action breeds clarity – the more you see properties, the more confident you'll become in recognizing a good deal.

Remember:

- **Done is Better Than Perfect:** Your first property might not be the ultimate dream investment. But getting started allows you to build a track record and gain experience. Don't be afraid to start small and learn as you go.
- **Learn from Every Deal:** Analyze each property you consider, successful bids or not. What did you learn about the

market, the neighborhood, or the negotiation process? How can you apply these insights to future decisions? Every interaction is a valuable learning opportunity.

- **Build a Team:** Surround yourself with a network of mentors, realtors, and financial advisors who can provide invaluable guidance and help you navigate complexities. A good team can fill knowledge gaps, offer different perspectives, and help you avoid costly mistakes.

The Investor's Edge: From Paralysis to Powerhouse

By overcoming analysis paralysis, you gain the "Investor's Edge." You become decisive, able to spot opportunities and act swiftly in a competitive market. Remember, successful investors aren't those who never make mistakes; they're the ones who learn, adapt, and keep moving forward. So, take a deep breath, set your goals, assemble your team, and embark on your property investment journey with confidence! Remember, knowledge is power, but action translates knowledge into wealth.

Chapter 16: Don't have the clear strategy

15 Property Investing Strategies

Welcome, investor! The property market beckons, brimming with potential. But where to begin? Without a clear strategy, this exciting venture can quickly become overwhelming. Fear not! This chapter will unveil 15 property investing strategies, empowering you to identify the path that aligns with your goals and resources.

Finding Your Fit

Think of property investment strategies as tools in a toolbox. A hammer excels at driving nails, but wouldn't work for sawing wood. Similarly, the perfect strategy hinges on your unique circumstances. Consider these factors:

- **Risk Tolerance:** Are you comfortable with higher risks for potentially greater rewards?
- **Time Commitment:** Can you dedicate significant time to active management, or prefer a more passive approach?
- **Financial Goals:** Is steady cash flow your priority, or long-term capital appreciation?
- **Budget:** How much capital can you invest initially, and are you comfortable with leverage (borrowing)?

15 Strategies to Explore

1. **Buy-to-Let (Rental Properties):** A classic strategy. You purchase a property and rent it out, generating income and potentially benefiting from long-term appreciation.
2. **Buy and Hold (Refinancing):** This long-term approach involves acquiring and holding onto properties, strategically refinancing to access equity and grow your portfolio.
3. **Flipping:** For the risk-tolerant and rehab-savvy, this involves

buying undervalued properties, renovating them to increase value, and selling them quickly for a profit.

4. **Rent-to-Own:** This caters to tenants who aspire to homeownership. You retain ownership while they rent, with a portion of their rent going towards eventual purchase.
5. **Air BnB Serviced Accommodation:** Transform a property into short-term rentals, ideal for tourists or business travelers. This requires active management but offers potentially high yields.
6. **Student Accommodation:** Target properties near universities or colleges. Student renters tend to be reliable, creating a steady income stream.
7. **Holiday Rentals:** Capitalize on seasonal tourism by owning property in desirable vacation destinations. Requires good management for turnovers and maintenance.
8. **Commercial Property:** Invest in office buildings, retail spaces, or industrial units. This offers potentially higher yields but comes with increased risk and complexities.
9. **AirBnb Rent to Rent:** Sublet other people's properties and make profit using their assets.
10. **Real Estate Investment Groups (REIGs):** Pool your resources with other investors to gain access to larger projects and benefit from expertise.
11. **Joint Ventures:** Partner with another investor to combine resources and expertise for mutually beneficial property deals.
12. **Development Projects:** For those with experience and capital, consider acquiring land and developing it for residential or commercial purposes. Offers high potential returns but comes with significant risk.
13. **Student Accommodation:** Investing into students accommodation and getting into agreements with universities.

14. **Crowdfunding:** Invest in property ventures alongside a crowd of online investors. Offers access to a wider range of opportunities but with potentially less control.
15. **Online Real Estate Platforms:** Facilitate investment in fractional shares of properties, allowing for lower initial investment and diversification.

Embrace the Exploration

This is not an exhaustive list! Research each strategy thoroughly, considering the entry and exit costs, tax implications, and ongoing management requirements. Talk to successful property investors, financial advisors, and real estate professionals.

Remember, the best strategy is the one that aligns with your goals, risk tolerance, and resources. So, grab your metaphorical toolbox, explore these strategies, and discover the perfect fit for building your property investment empire!

With Riches and Beyond programs we teach these strategies and offer specialized mentorship programs specifically focusing on market proof property investing.

More info at www.richesandbeyond.com[1]

1. http://www.richesandbeyond.com

Chapter 17: The Siren Song of Solely Relying on Banks:

A Property Investor's Pitfall

For many aspiring property investors, banks seem to offer the holy grail: financing. They hold the key to unlocking that dream property, the one that promises a future fortune. But relying solely on banks can be a dangerous gamble, a seductive melody that can lull you into a false sense of security. This chapter will explore the pitfalls of this approach and equip you with the knowledge to navigate a more strategic path.

The Allure of One-Stop Shopping:

Banks present a seemingly convenient solution. They assess your situation, provide a loan, and – ta-da! – you're a property owner. This one-stop shop can be tempting, especially for beginners. However, banks prioritize security, minimizing their risk. This translates to stringent lending criteria, often demanding high deposits and perfect credit scores. Many promising investments, particularly those requiring renovations or falling outside prime locations, fall outside these rigid parameters, leaving you locked out of potentially lucrative opportunities. Imagine a hidden gem in an up-and-coming neighborhood – a bank might deem it too risky, while a savvy investor with alternative funding can turn it into a goldmine.

Beyond the Loan: The Hidden Costs:

Banks are not financial advisors; their primary concern is getting their money back with interest. They might not consider crucial factors like property maintenance costs, potential vacancy periods, or market fluctuations. These hidden costs can quickly erode your profit margins, turning your dream investment into a financial burden. Let's say a bank approves your loan for a seemingly affordable fixer-upper. However, unforeseen repairs and unexpected vacancies could leave you scrambling to cover the mortgage while renovations drag on. With alternative financing, you might have more negotiation power to secure a loan with a buffer built-in for contingencies.

The Bank Doesn't Share Your Vision:

Your property journey is unique. You might envision a long-term buy-and-hold strategy or a value-add project with renovations. Banks, however, often focus on standardized loan products with fixed terms. This inflexibility can stifle your creativity and limit your ability to adapt your strategy as market conditions evolve. Perhaps you see an opportunity to convert a single-family home into a multi-unit rental property. A bank loan might not cater to such a specific niche, but a private lender with experience in that area could be a perfect fit.

Expanding Your Funding Arsenal: Alternative Avenues

Fortunately, the financial world is far broader than just banks. Here are some alternative avenues to explore, each with its own advantages and considerations:

- **Private lenders:** These individuals or entities offer more flexible options with potentially faster approvals, though often at higher interest rates. Conduct thorough due diligence before signing with a private lender, ensuring their reputation and terms align with your goals.
- **Hard money loans:** Ideal for quick turnaround situations like fixer-uppers, these short-term loans come with steep interest rates but can unlock valuable opportunities. They are best used strategically for properties that can be flipped quickly for a profit, allowing you to capitalize on a distressed market.
- **Joint ventures:** Partnering with other investors pools resources and expertise, allowing you to tackle projects

beyond your individual capabilities. Look for partners who complement your skillset and share your investment philosophy.

The Takeaway: Building a Robust Portfolio

Building a successful property portfolio requires a diversified approach. Banks can be a valuable tool, especially for established investors with a strong financial track record. However, they shouldn't be your only one. Educate yourself on alternative financing options, understand their pros and cons, and don't be afraid to get creative. By wielding a wider range of financial instruments, you'll gain the freedom and flexibility to pursue a broader range of lucrative property opportunities. Remember, successful property investors are those who can adapt, seize opportunities, and navigate an ever-changing market. By breaking free from the limitations of solely relying on banks, you'll be well on your way to building a robust and sustainable property portfolio that weathers any storm.

Chapter 18: Don't use OPM

Why Ignoring OPM Can Stall Your Portfolio

For many property investors, the dream starts with a single brick. But the reality is, building a substantial portfolio takes time, capital, and often, a strategic shift in thinking. One crucial concept that can propel even the most diligent investor forward is often overlooked: Other People's Money (OPM).

This chapter dives into the common misconception that property investment requires solely your own savings. We'll explore the power of OPM, the potential pitfalls to avoid, and how to leverage it effectively to supercharge your portfolio's growth.

The Allure of Self-Funding: A Slow and Steady Climb

The traditional approach to property investment involves diligently saving and using your own capital to acquire properties. There's a sense of accomplishment in financing everything yourself. However, this self-funded strategy has limitations:

- **Slow Growth:** Brick by painstaking brick, building wealth relies on the limited funds you can accumulate. This can significantly extend the time it takes to achieve your investment goals. Imagine a scenario where you diligently save $20,000 a year for a 20% down payment on a $100,000 property. By the time you acquire your second property, years would have passed, hindering your ability to capitalize on market opportunities or weather economic downturns.
- **Limited Opportunities:** Attractive properties often require significant capital. Without OPM, you might miss out on lucrative deals that could significantly elevate your portfolio's value. Perhaps a multi-unit apartment building with excellent rental potential comes on the market, but your self-funded approach restricts you to single-family homes. By leveraging OPM, you could seize this opportunity, increasing your cash flow and long-term returns.

The Magnifying Power of OPM: Exponential Growth

OPM refers to leveraging external funding sources to finance your property acquisitions. This opens a world of possibilities:

- **Amplified Buying Power:** Imagine being able to acquire multiple properties instead of just one, using a portion of your own capital alongside borrowed funds. This translates to a faster-growing portfolio and potentially higher returns. Consider a scenario where you have $50,000 saved for a down payment. With a traditional mortgage, you could acquire a single property. However, by using OPM strategically, you could leverage that $50,000 into two or even three properties, significantly accelerating your wealth creation.
- **Diversification:** OPM allows you to diversify your holdings across different property types and locations, mitigating risk and increasing your income streams. Perhaps you've been focused on residential properties in your local area. By strategically using OPM, you could expand your portfolio to include a vacation rental property in a tourist destination or a commercial property with a long-term lease agreement. This diversification helps mitigate risk by ensuring your income isn't solely reliant on one market or property type.

Examples of OPM in Action:

- **Mortgages:** This is the most common form of OPM. Banks lend you money to purchase a property, allowing you to control the asset while the loan is repaid.

- **Private Lenders:** These individuals or entities offer financing with potentially more flexible terms than traditional banks. They may be suitable for niche properties or quick acquisitions.
- **Hard Money Loans:** These short-term, high-interest loans are ideal for quick acquisitions that require renovation before resale. They are best used strategically due to the higher interest rates.

Mastering the Art of Leverage: Calculated Risks and Responsibilities

While OPM unlocks immense potential, it's not without its challenges:

- **Debt Management:** Carefully assess your ability to repay borrowed funds. Factor in potential fluctuations in rental income and market downturns. Don't overextend yourself; ensure your debt service coverage ratio (DSCR) is sufficient to handle your mortgage payments even if vacancy rates rise or rental income dips slightly.
- **Exit Strategy:** Clearly define how you'll generate returns to pay back the loan and achieve your investment goals. Will you be relying on rental income, property appreciation, or a combination of both? Having a clear exit strategy ensures you're not caught off guard when it's time to sell or refinance.
- **Risk Tolerance:** OPM magnifies both gains and losses. Ensure your risk tolerance aligns with the level of leverage you employ. If you're a conservative investor, using a lower percentage of OPM might be more suitable.

Utilizing OPM effectively requires a strategic mindset and responsible financial planning. Consult with financial advisors and experienced property investors to ensure you leverage OPM effectively and navigate the potential risks.

Building Your OPM Arsenal: Beyond Traditional Mortgages

While mortgages are a powerful OPM tool, there's a wider arsenal at your disposal:

House Hacking: House hacking involves living in one unit of a multi-unit property and renting out the others. This allows you to offset your living expenses with rental income, essentially using your tenants' money to help pay your mortgage.

- **Joint Ventures:** Partnering with other investors allows you to pool resources and access opportunities that might be out of reach individually. Clearly define roles, responsibilities, and profit-sharing structures to ensure a smooth and successful partnership.
- **Real Estate Investment Trusts (REITs):** These publicly traded companies allow you to invest in a portfolio of income-generating properties without the hassle of direct ownership. This provides a more passive approach to benefiting from real estate while leveraging the expertise of the REIT's management team.

Remember: OPM is a tool, and like any tool, it requires knowledge and skill to wield effectively. By understanding its potential and pitfalls, you can leverage OPM to become a more strategic and successful property investor, accelerating your path to achieving your financial goals.

The takeaway? Don't be afraid to get creative and explore the various ways to incorporate OPM into your investment strategy. With careful planning and responsible execution, OPM can be the fuel that propels your property portfolio to new heights.

Chapter 19: Not open minded to new information

Why Staying Open-Minded Fuels Property Investment Success

The world of property investment is a dynamic landscape. New trends emerge, regulations shift, and technology disrupts traditional methods. Investors who thrive in this environment aren't just those with deep pockets or a knack for picking perfect properties. The secret weapon of many successful investors is a surprisingly simple yet powerful trait: **open-mindedness.**

This chapter explores the dangers of clinging to outdated information and the immense benefits of embracing a growth mindset in property investment. We'll delve into how staying open-minded allows you to identify new opportunities, adapt to changing markets, and ultimately, build a more resilient and successful portfolio.

The Pitfall of Confirmation Bias: Sticking to What You Know

Many investors fall victim to confirmation bias, a cognitive trap where we subconsciously seek out information that confirms our existing beliefs and disregard anything that contradicts them. This can be detrimental in property investment:

- **Missed Opportunities:** Clinging to outdated strategies can blind you to emerging trends. Perhaps you've always focused on traditional single-family homes, dismissing the potential of co-living spaces or vacation rentals. By staying open to new investment avenues, you might uncover lucrative opportunities that align with changing demographics and market demands.
- **Ignoring Risks:** Being close-minded to potential risks can lead to costly mistakes. For example, if you're convinced a particular location is guaranteed to appreciate, you might overlook potential infrastructure disruptions or environmental concerns that could negatively impact property values.
- **Limited Growth:** A closed mind restricts your ability to learn and adapt. New technologies like virtual tours and online property management platforms can revolutionize how you handle your portfolio. By staying open to these innovations, you can streamline processes, save time, and potentially improve returns.

Embracing New Information: Igniting Your Investment Journey

Here's how staying open-minded can propel you forward:

- **Constant Learning:** Successful investors are voracious learners. Attend industry events, network with other investors, and actively seek out new information. Podcasts, webinars, and online resources can provide valuable insights into evolving market trends, investment strategies, and legal frameworks.
- **Challenging Assumptions:** Don't be afraid to question your existing beliefs and investment strategies. Research alternative approaches, consult with mentors, and analyze real-world case studies to broaden your perspective.
- **Adaptability:** Markets are fluid, and what worked yesterday might not be optimal today. Be prepared to adjust your strategies based on changing demographics, economic factors, and new regulations. This agility allows you to capitalize on emerging opportunities and mitigate potential risks.

Remember: Open-mindedness doesn't equate to recklessness. It's about fostering an environment for continuous learning and critical thinking. This allows you to make informed decisions based on a well-rounded understanding of the market, not just your existing biases.

Open Your Mind, Open Your Portfolio's Potential

By staying open-minded, you'll be better equipped to navigate the ever-evolving world of property investment. Here are some practical ways to cultivate this critical mindset:

- **Seek Out Diverse Perspectives:** Network with investors from different backgrounds and experiences. Talk to industry experts, attend conferences, and join online communities where you can exchange ideas and learn from others. Look for those who have achieved success through unconventional approaches or in niche markets. Their experiences can broaden your understanding of what's possible.
- **Embrace New Technologies:** Explore how technology can streamline your property management tasks and potentially increase your returns. Be open to learning new software and platforms that could revolutionize your approach. Consider virtual reality tours that allow potential tenants to explore properties remotely or artificial intelligence-powered tools that can automate tenant screening and rent collection.
- **Challenge Yourself:** Step outside your comfort zone. Consider a new investment strategy or explore a different property type. Perhaps delve into crowdfunding platforms for real estate or research the potential of student housing in a growing university town. While calculated risks are essential, ensure you conduct thorough research before venturing into unfamiliar territory.
- **Travel with Open Eyes:** Your travels can be a valuable source of inspiration. Observe how different cultures utilize and manage properties. Are there unique architectural styles or

community living arrangements that could be adapted to your local market?

Open-mindedness is not a passive state; it's an ongoing commitment to learning and adapting. By embracing this approach, you equip yourself with the tools needed to make informed decisions, identify lucrative opportunities, and build a resilient and successful property portfolio for the long term. So, keep your eyes peeled, stay curious, and watch your property investment journey reach new heights. As the ancient proverb goes, "The only true wisdom is in knowing you know nothing." By acknowledging the limitations of your existing knowledge and embracing the potential for continuous learning, you position yourself for long-term success in the dynamic world of property investment.

Chapter 20: Give up at the first obstacle

Why Persistence is Your Property Investment Secret Weapon

The allure of property investment? It's simple: turning a quick profit and building wealth brick by brick (or should we say, house by house?). But the reality of a successful portfolio involves more than just a lucky deal. It's about perseverance, the determination to push through setbacks and navigate the inevitable obstacles that come with navigating the property market. This chapter dives into the critical mistake of giving up at the first hurdle and explores how cultivating persistence can unlock long-term success in property investment.

Giving Up on Gold: Why Short-Term Thinking Limits Your Growth

Many novice investors approach property with a "get rich quick" mentality. They envision flipping a house in a few months and walking away with a hefty profit. While this scenario might happen occasionally, it's not a sustainable strategy for building a thriving portfolio. The reality is, property investment is a marathon, not a sprint. Here's why giving up at the first sign of trouble hinders your long-term goals:

- **Missed Opportunities:** The property market is cyclical. Prices might dip momentarily, leading to discouragement. However, abandoning the market during these downturns can mean missing out on potentially lucrative acquisitions. Persistent investors understand that these cycles are temporary and view them as opportunities to acquire properties at a discount.
- **Loss of Valuable Lessons:** Every challenge encountered is a learning experience. Perhaps you misjudged renovations costs

or faced unexpected delays with permits. These setbacks, while frustrating in the moment, equip you with valuable knowledge. By giving up, you lose the opportunity to learn from these experiences and become a more informed investor in the future.

- **Building a Network Takes Time:** Successful property investment often relies on a network of professionals - brokers, contractors, property managers. Building strong relationships takes time and consistent interaction. Quitting after one negative experience might mean missing out on valuable connections that could streamline your future endeavors.

Persistence Pays Off: Cultivating the Mindset of a Champion Investor

So, how do you develop the unwavering determination required for long-term success? Here are some key strategies:

- **Define Your "Why":** Having a clear purpose fuels your motivation. Are you aiming to create financial security for your family? Secure a passive income stream for retirement? A strong "why" becomes your anchor, reminding you of your long-term goals when faced with short-term challenges.
- **Embrace Calculated Risks:** Playing it too safe can limit your growth potential. While recklessness is unwise, calculated risks can lead to significant rewards. Research opportunities thoroughly, understand the potential pitfalls, and don't be afraid to step outside your comfort zone occasionally. Remember, even the most successful investors have encountered setbacks – what matters most is how they learn and adapt from them.

- **Focus on the Journey:** Building a portfolio is a process full of milestones, big and small. Don't wait for the "big win" to celebrate your achievements. Successfully negotiating a lease agreement, securing a reliable tenant, or completing a minor renovation are all steps forward. Acknowledge your progress, no matter how incremental.
- **Learn from the Masters:** Seek out mentors and study the journeys of successful property investors. Read their biographies, listen to podcasts, and attend industry events. Learn from their experiences, both positive and negative, and glean valuable insights into navigating challenges and capitalizing on opportunities.
- **Build a Support System:** Surround yourself with positive individuals who believe in your vision. Connect with other property investors, form a mastermind group, or find a mentor who can offer guidance and encouragement throughout your journey.

Beyond Persistence: Embracing the Rollercoaster Ride

Think of property investment as a rollercoaster ride, not a smooth cruise. There will be exhilarating highs of successful acquisitions and frustrating dips during market downturns or unexpected repairs. Persistence isn't just about gritting your teeth through challenges; it's about embracing the entire journey, with all its twists and turns.

Here's how to thrive on the rollercoaster:

- **Develop Emotional Intelligence:** The property market can evoke a range of emotions. Learn to manage your emotions effectively. Don't let euphoria cloud your judgment during buying sprees, and don't let discouragement lead to impulsive decisions during market slumps. Maintain a level head and make calculated decisions based on sound research and strategic planning.

- **Embrace Continuous Learning:** The landscape of property investment is constantly evolving. New technologies emerge, regulations shift, and market trends fluctuate. Persistent investors are lifelong learners. Stay abreast of industry trends, attend educational seminars, and network with experienced investors to continuously expand your knowledge base.

Adapt and Evolve: Rigidity is the enemy of success in property investment. Be prepared to adapt your strategies based on changing market conditions and unforeseen circumstances. Perhaps you initially focused on single-family homes in your local area. However, persistent investors might identify a growing demand for student housing near a newly established university. By adapting their strategies and venturing into new markets, they can capitalize on these emerging opportunities.

Remember, persistence is a superpower in the world of property investment. It equips you with the resilience to navigate challenges, the wisdom to learn from setbacks, and the unwavering determination to keep moving forward towards your long-term goals. So, the next time you encounter an obstacle, don't let it deter you. Embrace the challenge, learn from it, and channel your inner persistence. With unwavering resolve and a strategic approach, you'll be well on your way to building a thriving property portfolio that fuels your financial success for years to come.

Chapter 21: Thinking it's a get rich quick venture

Why Property Investment is a Marathon, Not a Sprint

The dream of property investment is seductive: turning a quick profit, building wealth with every brick laid. Social media and reality TV paint a rosy picture of flipping houses and amassing instant fortunes. However, the reality of successful property investment is far more nuanced. This chapter dismantles the myth of property as a "get rich quick" scheme and explores why a long-term, strategic approach is the key to building a sustainable and rewarding portfolio.

The Allure and the Illusion: Why Short-Term Thinking Doesn't Deliver

There's no denying the potential for profit in property. However, focusing solely on quick flips can be a recipe for disappointment. Here's why a "get rich quick" mentality hinders your long-term goals:

- **Market Fluctuations:** The property market is cyclical. While there are opportunities to capitalize on hot markets and rising prices, there will inevitably be downturns. A "get rich quick" mentality might lead you to sell prematurely during dips, missing out on long-term appreciation.
- **Underestimating Costs:** Renovations, unexpected repairs, and ongoing maintenance can quickly eat into your profit margins. Focusing solely on the sale price and neglecting these ongoing costs can lead to financial strain and dashed dreams of instant wealth.
- **Neglecting Cash Flow:** Successful property investors understand the power of rental income. Chasing quick flips ignores the potential for steady, passive income generated through well-managed rentals.

Building Wealth Brick by Brick: The Power of Long-Term Strategy

So, how do you transition from a short-term mindset to a long-term vision? Here are some key strategies:

- **Define Your Goals:** Are you aiming for long-term capital appreciation? Building a portfolio that generates passive income? Retiring early and living off rental income? Having a clear vision helps you develop a strategy tailored to your specific goals.
- **Embrace the Buy-and-Hold Mentality:** While flipping houses can be profitable, building wealth in property often involves a buy-and-hold approach. This allows you to benefit from long-term appreciation, inflation-hedging, and generate consistent rental income.
- **Focus on Value Investing:** Look for properties with strong fundamentals and growth potential. Target locations with a growing population, good schools, and increasing job opportunities. These factors contribute to long-term value appreciation and a higher chance of your properties remaining rented throughout economic cycles.
- **Become a Property Management Pro:** Develop the skills to manage your properties effectively. Learn how to screen tenants, handle maintenance requests, maximize your rental income, and stay compliant with legal regulations. This knowledge empowers you to control your cash flow, build long-term wealth, and potentially avoid the need for expensive property managers.

The Marathon Mindset: Essential Traits for Long-Term Success

Building a successful property portfolio requires a specific set of skills and characteristics that go beyond the thrill of a quick sale:

- **Patience:** Building wealth in property takes time and discipline. Don't expect overnight success. Be patient, focus on long-term goals, and enjoy the journey of building a sustainable portfolio that weathers market fluctuations.
- **Discipline:** Property investment requires calculated risks and informed decisions, not impulsive purchases based on market hype or emotional attachment to a particular property. Develop a disciplined approach based on thorough research, market analysis, and a long-term vision.
- **Financial Literacy:** Understanding financial metrics like cash flow, return on investment (ROI), capitalization rate, and debt-to-equity ratio is crucial for making informed investment decisions. Educate yourself on these financial concepts to ensure you're making sound financial choices throughout your investment journey.
- **Continuous Learning:** The property market is constantly evolving with new technologies, legal regulations, and economic factors impacting investment strategies. Stay up-to-date on industry trends by attending seminars, networking with experienced investors, and reading industry publications. This continuous learning ensures you're adapting your strategies to optimize your portfolio's performance.

Beyond the Finish Line: Building a Legacy

Think of property investment as a marathon, not a sprint. The goal is to create a sustainable source of wealth that can provide financial security for yourself and future generations.

Here's how to ensure your investment journey goes the distance:

- **Diversify Your Portfolio:** Don't put all your eggs in one basket. Spread your investments across different property types (residential, commercial, industrial) and locations to mitigate risks and maximize potential returns. Consider factors like vacancy rates, rental income potential, and long-term growth prospects for each location.

Build a Strong Team: Surround yourself with experienced professionals: real estate agents, property managers, financial advisors, and potentially legal counsel. Their expertise can guide you through complex transactions, ensure you're making sound decisions, and free up your time to focus on acquiring more properties and growing your portfolio.

- **Enjoy the Journey:** Building a successful property portfolio can be a rewarding experience. Take pride in your accomplishments, celebrate milestones (like acquiring a new property or securing a long-term tenant), and learn from setbacks. Remember, property investment is a marathon, but it can also be a thrilling journey filled with learning, growth, and the satisfaction of building a lasting legacy for yourself and your loved ones.

Property investment, when approached with a long-term strategy and a commitment to continuous learning, can be a powerful tool for building wealth and achieving financial security. By abandoning the "get rich quick" mentality and embracing the marathon mindset, you'll be well-equipped to navigate market fluctuations, make informed decisions, and build a portfolio that delivers sustainable returns for years to come. So, lace up your running shoes, develop your long-term vision, and embark on the rewarding journey of property investment.

Chapter 22: Get talked out of venture by friends and family

Why Ignoring Naysayers Can Propel Your Property Investment Journey

The path to property investment success is rarely paved with unanimous support. Family and friends, often with good intentions, might express doubts or anxieties about your investment plans. This chapter explores the reasons behind these well-meaning interventions and equips you with the tools to navigate them effectively. Remember, sometimes the most important voice to listen to is your own, fueled by research, a well-defined strategy, and a healthy dose of self-belief.

The Chorus of Doubt: Why Loved Ones Might Discourage Your Investment Dreams

While their intentions may be pure, loved ones can sometimes become obstacles on your investment journey. Here's why they might express negativity:

- **Fear of the Unknown:** For those unfamiliar with property investment, the complexities and potential risks can seem daunting. They might project their anxieties onto you, urging you to stick with the "safe" path, even if it hinders your long-term financial goals. Perhaps your parents instilled in you a strong aversion to debt, and the idea of leveraging mortgages for property acquisition seems risky.
- **Personal Biases:** Negative past experiences with property investment, either personal or through stories they've heard, might cloud their judgment. They might recount tales of a friend who lost money on a flip or a relative who struggled with a demanding tenant. These anecdotal experiences, while valid, shouldn't overshadow the potential rewards of a well-planned and strategically executed investment strategy.
- **Misinformation:** Often, advice comes from a place of limited knowledge. Friends or family might base their opinions on outdated information gleaned from headlines or watercooler conversations, not on current market trends and sound investment principles. They might be unaware of the various property types, investment strategies, and risk-mitigation techniques available to modern investors.

Drowning Out the Noise: Charting Your Course with Confidence

So, how do you navigate the chorus of doubt and pursue your property investment goals with steadfast resolve? Here are some key strategies:

- **Do Your Research:** Knowledge is power. Educate yourself on property investment principles, market trends, and financial metrics. The more you know, the more confidently you can address concerns and demonstrate that you've made informed decisions. Explore resources beyond anecdotal stories – delve into industry publications, attend educational seminars, and connect with experienced investors to gain a well-rounded understanding of the market and potential investment strategies.
- **Develop a Compelling Investment Plan:** Don't rely on blind optimism. Create a detailed investment plan outlining your goals, target properties, acquisition strategies, and financial projections. This plan not only clarifies your vision but also demonstrates your commitment and preparedness. Consider factors like your risk tolerance, desired cash flow, and long-term investment horizon. Show your loved ones that you've approached this venture thoughtfully and have a clear roadmap for success.
- **Seek Out Mentorship:** Connect with experienced property investors who can provide guidance and support. Seek mentors who share your long-term vision and can offer practical advice based on their real-world experiences. Look for individuals who can answer your questions, address your concerns, and provide valuable insights into navigating the complexities of the market.

- **Focus on Your "Why":** Remind yourself of your overarching goals for investing in property. Are you building wealth for your family's future, securing a passive income stream for retirement, or aiming for financial freedom to pursue your passions? Having a clear purpose fuels your motivation and allows you to stay focused even when faced with negativity from others. Visualize the life you're working towards, and let that vision guide your decisions and bolster your determination.
- **Communicate Effectively:** Talk to your loved ones openly and honestly about your investment plans. Address their concerns directly, share your research findings, and explain the potential rewards. Often, negativity stems from a lack of understanding. Open communication can bridge the gap and foster their support. Explain the steps you're taking to mitigate risks, the potential returns you're aiming for, and how this investment aligns with your long-term financial goals.

Remember, you are the captain of your investment journey. Don't let the well-meaning, but potentially uninformed, opinions of others derail your carefully charted course.

Beyond "Yes, But...": Building a Support System That Empowers You

While some friends and family might express doubts, others can become invaluable allies on your investment journey. Here's how to cultivate a supportive network:

- **Connect with Like-Minded Individuals:** Seek out other property investors. Join online communities, attend industry events, or find a mastermind group where you can share experiences, learn from each other's successes and challenges, and hold each other accountable for achieving your goals. Surrounding yourself with individuals who understand the intricacies of property investment and share your passion for building wealth through real estate can provide encouragement, motivation, and valuable insights.
- **Seek Out Mentors:** As mentioned earlier, mentorship is a powerful tool. Find experienced investors who can guide you through the complexities of the market, offer strategic advice, and answer your questions. Look for individuals whose investment philosophies align with yours and who are willing to share their knowledge and experience to help you navigate the path to success.
- **Turn Skeptics into Allies:** Sometimes, by effectively communicating your plans and addressing their concerns, you can turn naysayers into allies. Share your investment strategy, explain the steps you're taking to mitigate risks, and highlight the potential rewards. Their initial skepticism might stem from a lack of understanding. Open communication and a well-defined plan can bridge the gap and earn their support, or at least, their understanding of your goals.

Remember, property investment is a journey, not a solo expedition. Building a strong support system of mentors, peers, and even some well-informed loved ones can provide invaluable guidance, encouragement, and a sense of community as you navigate the exciting, and sometimes challenging, world of property investment.

The key takeaway? While the opinions of loved ones can sometimes create doubt, don't let them silence your inner voice. By educating yourself, developing a sound strategy, and surrounding yourself with a supportive network, you can confidently steer your own course towards property investment success. So, chart your path, address concerns with knowledge and reason, and embark on your investment journey with unwavering belief in your vision and the power of well-planned property investment.

Just as there are several ways to succeed in property investing there are many mistakes that can be made also.

It's time to build your Riches and Beyond!

With Riches and Beyond programs we have changed lives of over 40 000 students

and helped them raise over R500 million for their property deals. Also, our programs are SETA and QCTO accredited with our very own TV Show " THE PROPERTY GAME" airing on The Home Channel, where our students share their success stories and strategies learned from us.

We have students who started as total beginners, learned the right way and

already reaping the benefits of this knowledge. Employees who started building

their property portfolio in their spare time have seen the clear path to success.

Also, retired folks who decided that it's never too late to start, finally started

benefiting with their cash flowing properties.

Our students are involved in multiple projects, buy to lets, multi lets, capital flips,

buying at the auctions and multimillion rand developments.

None of this would be possible if they didn't say yes to their greatness, learned

from their own mistakes and decided to do something different.

I hope this guide has given you more insight on how not to do things and hope that

you will learn from my mistakes. While mistakes were needed to happen for me to

learn something, I wish I had this guide and my mentor 14 years ago when I started. I am pretty sure this approach would have saved me time and *money*.

It happened to the most of us who lacked knowledge and were uninformed.

What's important, though, is understanding the process, strategy and the team of

people you need to do avoid costly mistakes. Having the right people in your

Property Mastermind Group will help you identify the right steps to take, and with

the help of the right mentor success is just around the corner.

See you on the other side of success! – Milan Milosevic

Visit www.richesandbeyond.com and browse through our various training streams

that have been created to provide you with insider knowledge on the South African and global property market.

ABOUT THE AUTHOR

From Immigrant to Real Estate Guru: Milan's Journey to Success

Milan's story is one of perseverance and a burning desire to break free from the mold.

Raised in Serbia with a strong work ethic instilled by his parents, he dreamt of more than just a comfortable retirement. This ambition led him to the USA, where he met his wife, Sylvia.

Despite language barriers, Milan's determination to succeed never wavered. Early ventures into property investment proved challenging, highlighting the importance of mentorship. Realizing the value of learning from those who had already achieved success, Milan sought guidance from a multimillionaire mentor. This marked a turning point, shifting his focus from simply working hard to working smart alongside experts.

Today, Milan is a multifaceted figure: international speaker, mentor, entrepreneur, and investor. A serial entrepreneur with a passion for real estate and empowering young minds, he co-founded Riches and Beyond alongside his (now former) wife and a team of specialists. This program empowers students worldwide to achieve financial independence through knowledge and strategic application. The impact is undeniable – thousands of lives transformed and over R500 million ($30 million) raised for student deals, a testament to the power of knowledge and ambition.

Driven by a desire to help others achieve financial freedom, Milan advocates for the right mindset, knowledge, and unwavering passion. He firmly believes that success hinges on the right knowledge, proven systems, and experienced guidance.

Beyond his professional achievements, Milan cherishes time spent traveling with his children, Stefan and Jasmine, and finds solace in his Johannesburg home (Fourways).

Milan's story is an inspiration, a roadmap to success built on self-belief, strategic learning, and a commitment to empower others.

"Having a mentor was the best decision I have ever made!

Someone to hold you accountable and guide you along the way

was that missing link I needed to have to reach the long-desired success."

- Milan Milosevic

About the Author

Co-Founder of Riches and Beyond, a leading property education company in South Africa, Founder of Millionaire Speakers, host of Riches and Beyond and a Millionaire Speakers podcast, Editor in Chief of Millionaire Speakers Magazine, International speaker, entrepreneur, speakers coach, property mentor and a Amazon best-selling author of "Cracking the Rich Code" - Book endorsed by Tony Robbins.

Milan left his country Serbia in 2005 as a college dropout, being broke and could barely speak English. Over time he learned from the top property investors and speakers, got himself different mentors, and started learning about property and business.

After seeing massive success in the property investment business, Milan co-founded Riches and Beyond, now a leading South African Property education company with over 50 000 students. Riches and Beyond have partnered up with top residential and commercial developers in South Africa and created a powerful program that transformed the lives of aspiring and seasoned property investors.

Milan is also the founder of the Millionaire speakers program which teaches politicians, ceos, entrepreneurs and aspiring speakers how to build a business to 7-8 figures with your story and speaking. Being an international speaker for the last 15 years and having done over 1 000 live presentations as well as hundreds of webinars, he has learned from the greats like Robert Kiyosaki, Les Brown, Lisa Nichols, Jim Francis, Bob Proctor, Michel Beckwith and has spoken internationally in the US, UK, Dubai, and South Africa!

Featured in Your Business Magazine, Entrepreneur Magazine, Powerhouse Speakers, and several business podcasts.

Milan is passionate about transferring knowledge to others and empowering aspiring entrepreneurs.

"The true secret in business is in building relationships and providing enormous value." - Milan Milosevic

Read more at https://millionairespeakers.com.

www.ingramcontent.com/pod-product-compliance
Lightning Source LLC
LaVergne TN
LVHW022102200926
848481LV00003B/1032
* 9 7 9 8 2 2 4 4 6 8 6 6 9 *